EVERYDAY BUDDHA

A CONTEMPORARY RENDERING OF THE
BUDDHIST CLASSIC, THE DHAMMAPADA

BOOKS

WINCHESTER UK
NEW YORK USA

Copyright © 2005 O Books
O Books is an imprint of The Bothy, John Hunt Publishing Ltd.,
Deershot Lodge, Park Lane, Ropley, Hants, SO24 0BE, UK
office@johnhunt-publishing.com
www.O-books.net

Distribution in:
UK
Orca Book Services
orders@orcabookservices.co.uk
Tel: 01202 665432 Fax: 01202 666219 Int. code (44)

USA AND CANADA
NBN
custserv@nbnbooks.com
Tel: 1 800 462 6420 Fax: 1 800 338 4550

AUSTRALIA
Brumby Books
sales@brumbybooks.com
Tel: 61 3 9761 5535 Fax: 61 3 9761 7095

NEW ZEALAND
Peaceful Living
books@peaceful-living.co.nz
Tel: 64 7 57 18105 Fax: 64 7 57 18513

SINGAPORE
STP
davidbuckland@tlp.com.sg
Tel: 65 6276 Fax: 65 6276 7119

SOUTH AFRICA
Alternative Books
altbook@global.co.za
Tel: 27 011 792 7730 Fax: 27 011 972 7787

Design: BookDesign™, London

ISBN 1 905047 30 4

A CIP catalogue record for this book is available from the
British Library.

Printed in the USA by Maple-Vail Manufacturing Group

EVERYDAY BUDDHA

A CONTEMPORARY RENDERING OF THE BUDDHIST CLASSIC, THE DHAMMAPADA

BY
KARMA YONTEN SENGE
LAWRENCE R. ELLYARD

FOREWORD BY
HIS HOLINESS THE 14TH DALAI LAMA

CONTENTS

THE DALAI LAMA

AT my time of life, I have accumulated enough experience to be completely confident that the teachings of the Buddha are both relevant and useful to humanity. If you put them into practice, it is certain that not only you but others', too, will benefit. This is surely true of other faiths too, but I have also come to the conclusion that whether or not people are religious believers does not matter much. Far more important is that they be good human beings. That is something that can be achieved through constant familiarity and training with positive states of mind.

Through training, we can change; we can transform ourselves. Within Buddhist practice there are various methods of trying to sustain a calm mind when some disturbing event takes place. Through repeated practice of these methods we can reach a point where a disturbance may occur, but the negative effects on our mind remain on the surface, like the waves that may ripple on the surface of an ocean but don't have much effect deep down. But this is achieved through steady practice; it does not happen overnight.

The *Dhammapada* is a handbook of practical ethics, that may be of interest and benefit, whether you are Buddhist or not. But more than that, as a collection of verses that consist of statements and advice directly attributed to the Buddha, it represents a succinct summary of the Buddhist path.

Derived from the ancient Pali canon, the *Dhammapada* was not translated into Tibetan until relatively recently. However, another work, the *Udanavarga*, translated from the Sanskrit, contains many corresponding verses and was one of the six primary scriptures of the Kadampa tradition founded in eleventh century Tibet. The early Kadampa masters adopted an approach to the spiritual life based on an open-minded practice of hearing, contemplation and meditation. This meant that whatever they learned through study, hearing and contemplation was integrated into their mind-streams and, as far as possible, was applied in actual practice.

It is said that bringing about discipline within your mind is the essence of the Buddha's teaching. This is because a disciplined mind leads to happiness and an undisciplined mind leads to suffering. The *Dhammapada*, like the *Udanavarga*, describes a path of ethical behaviour that is a feature of this kind of inner discipline that leads to a happier existence. It includes advice suitable for everyone, whether they are beginners or advanced practitioners of Buddhism or people who simply seek a path to happiness. I am pleased that Karma Yonten Senge has made this modern rendering of the Dhammapada in English. I offer my prayers that readers who will study this will be successful in putting the advice it contains into practice.

THE DALAI LAMA

INTRODUCTION TO
EVERYDAY BUDDHA

Everyday Buddha is a contemporary rendering of the Buddhist classic, *The Dhammapada*. Any person who has ever reflected upon what it means to be human can profit from this source of wisdom. Not just a book to read from cover to cover, *Everyday Buddha* can be read and re-read as a guide upon the seekers path. For *The Dhammapada* is a lamp. It is a treasure trove of pure wisdom that has something to offer to everyone.

The Dhammapada is one of the thirty-one books which comprise the Tipitaka, the original Pali texts which contain the quintessence of the Buddha's Teachings. Of these texts, *The Dhammapada* is contained within the Khuddaka-Nikaya (Shorter Discourses) section of the Sutta Pitaka (Basket of Discourses). These sayings of the Buddha (563-483 B.C.), offer a rich tapestry of spiritual teachings and reflections of the spiritual path. More than just a collection of Buddhist sayings, the Dhammapada's message is timeless and crosses all cultural boundaries. It offers the reader a constant source of inspiration, reflection and companionship upon the path.

Surprisingly, the original Pali version was not spoken by the Buddha in its present form. Three months after the Buddha's passing his most devout disciples assembled at the First Convocation to rehearse and record the poetic utterances of the Buddha. These teachings were subsequently arranged and recorded and later became the treatise, named *The Dhammapada*. The original Pali text was recorded for the first time in the 1st Century before Christ in Ceylon (Sri Lanka). Consisting of 423 verses and arranged by topic into 26 chapters, these sayings were said to have been uttered by the Buddha on approximately 300 occasions to suit the temperaments of his listeners during his extensive teaching career which lasted forty five years. In total, the historical Buddha gave 84,000 teachings on the nature of Mind and the path of the Middle Way. These teachings were later categorized into the three main streams of Buddhism that we find in the world today, these being the vehicles of the *Hinayana*, (lesser vehicle) the *Mahayana*, (great vehicle) and the *Vajrayana*, (diamond vehicle).

Although a popular text among the Theravada (Hinayana) tradition, *The Dhammapada* holds a special place within the teachings of all Buddhist vehicles.

In order to more fully appreciate the background from where these teachings first arose, the following is a brief account of the life and path of the historical Buddha.

The Buddha was an Indian prince of the Sakya clan who was born approximately 560 BC. His family name was Gotama and his given name was Siddhartha. His family ruled part of northern India as well as part of what is today Nepal.
As Siddhartha was growing up, he received the finest education of the day. He was extremely bright and excelled in all of his studies.

Before his birth the king requested a divination and the outcome stated that he would either become a great ruler or a great religious teacher. The king, desiring an heir to his throne and with plans for Siddhartha to become a great emperor who, he hoped, would one day rule all of India, made certain that the young prince lead a life sheltered from the sorrows of this world.

In an attempt to prevent the prophecy, Siddhartha's life in the palace was filled with every kind of worldly pleasure and luxury.

Siddhartha was later married and in due course fathered a son. He lived amidst the splendour of the court for many years, yet something was missing. Curious to what lay beyond the palace walls he sought to know the world.

As the story was related, Siddhartha ventured outside the palace walls and encountered four sights: an old person who was crippled with age, a person riddled with sickness, a dead body being carried to the burning grounds, and a holy man with nothing more than a begging bowl and the loin cloth he was standing in.

These experiences filled Siddhartha with urgent questions in his mind. What is the meaning of life? Why do we suffer from old age, sickness and death? Is there a way to be free of this?

Realizing the luxury of the court could not give him the answers to his questions, he secretly left the palace one night in search of spiritual teachers who might.

For the next six years, Siddhartha studied with any teacher he could find and followed the arduous practices of the forest ascetics. It was considered that only through the extremes of harsh practices and depriving the senses of that body that realization could be achieved. Yet despite the years of self-mortification, he was no nearer the truth.

From the extremes of spiritual asceticism to the worldly pleasures of the life of a prince, Siddhartha had experienced the two extremes of desire and discipline.

At last he realised that the path to freedom could not be

found outside of himself, he resolved to find the answers. One night he decided to sit under a Bodhi tree and not leave until he knew the truth beyond all things. Though observing his mind through deep meditation he suddenly realised the meaning of birth and death, the meaning of existence and his minds' relationship to all existence. Like waking up from a deep sleep, he awoke to the truth. It is said that upon his enlightenment he uttered these words:

> *"Through countless weary lives*
> *I have sought the builder of this house*
> *and could not find him.*
> *Now, I have found you, O Builder,*
> *and you shall build no more.*
> *The rafters are broken,*
> *the ridge pole is shattered.*
> *I have beaten out desire*
> *and my mind is now free!"*

- The Dhammapada: Chapter 11, verses 153-154.

After his enlightenment and much contemplation he decided to share his insights with whomever would listen. It is said that his first teachings were given in Bodhgaya, Varanasi. Here, Siddhartha, or whom many were now calling him – the Tathagata (the one who has gone beyond), first gave the famous teachings on The Four Noble Truths.

The first being: the Truth of Suffering.

That throughout all of conditioned existence there is suffering in the form of old age, sickness and death and our minds are constantly filled with desire. The pain of losing what one likes, and the suffering caused by the things we do not like. To live is to suffer.

The second truth being: the Truth of the Origin of Suffering. The second noble truth states that our suffering has a cause. This cause is the existence of desire, ignorance and attachment. We constantly crave pleasure. We live in the past or are living in the future and continually thirst to be free of our current situation. All of these factors bind us to cyclic existence.

The third truth is that there is a way out of suffering, meaning there are methods to remove these causes. By utilizing the methods of a Buddha, we can transcend our sorrow and find a way that leads to ultimate happiness.

The fourth truth is that of the eightfold noble path. The methods that lead to the cessation of suffering. By following these eight steps, one can know a way that goes beyond suffering.

The following eight steps show the way to liberation.

1.   The first being the path of Right View: Without a

proper understanding of the nature of our problems we can do little to remedy the cause. Therefore we should strive to know the nature of our minds, recognise the interconnectedness of all that lives and to closely examine our motives and needs. By understanding the Four Noble Truths, we have the ability to understanding the non-individuality of all existence.

2. The second is the path of Right Thought. It matters how we think, because many thoughts are based on confusion, misunderstanding and prejudice. Therefore one should resolve to follow a path of right action, including good will, and not harming sentient beings.

3. The third path is that of Right Speech, recognising the value of non-harmful speech and avoiding lying, slander and gossip. Instead, one nurtures communication which is constructive, and life giving. This includes the speech in our minds about others and ourselves.

4. The fourth being Correct Conduct. To avoid actions which are in conflict with the cultivation of ethical and moral behaviour. The things that we do should be in accord with the benefit of all beings.

5. The fifth path is the path of Right Livelihood. To recognise the importance of a livelihood which

supports the path of Right Livelihood. It matters what we do; therefore one should avoid a vocation that causes harm to others or the environment.

6.   The sixth path is the path of Right Effort. To bring conscious effort into all that we do. The sixth path is a path of determination to do ones best by doing activities which are wholesome and avoiding activities which are unwholesome.

7.   The seventh path is that of Right Mindfulness. This path includes attention to the needs of our body, thoughts, emotions and mind. With proper awareness one is in control of ones' actions; one is also in the present moment and can see how things really are, not give into expectations and projections from the past or future.

8.   The eighth path is the path of Right Concentration. This is the training of the mind through meditation. By bringing concentrated effort to the mind for the practice of meditation and contemplation, one is able to achieve one pointed focus that results in a calm and tranquil mind.

By following these eight steps one gains steady insight into the nature of one's own mind. With careful attention and practice, the Buddha taught that these eight steps bring about four sublime states – benevolence, compassion, sympathetic joy and equanimity.

> *The way is the eightfold noble path.*
> *The truth is the four noble truths.*
> *The Master is free from craving*
> *and has eyes to see.*

> *This is the right way;*
> *the way that leads to liberation,*
> *the way that opens your eyes,*
> *the way to follow.*

> *The one who knows this path*
> *outwits sorrow.*

- The Dhammapada: Chapter 20, verses 273, 274, 275

Although the teachings of the Buddha are vast and contain hundreds of teachings on the nature of Mind, nearly all of them can be traced to one of these eight steps.

When we examine the original Pali text, the poems of *The Dhammapada* were written in verse consisting of four and six-line stanzas. These stanzas hold a distinctive rhythm, which when translated from Pali into English are somewhat lost. The task of translating this rendering into a modern interpretation, while still holding true to this rhythm, was challenging. This rendering is not supposed to be viewed as an official scholarly work. Rather, it is an interpretation of a timeless classic presented in this way so that it might reach a wider general audience. One should bear this in mind when making comparisons to more traditional translations.

There are many versions of *the Dhammapada* in print today and some of these renderings have been the source of inspiration for this rendering. The source of these versions can be found in the Bibliography at the end of this book.

In this modern rendering the Author has attempted, without straying greatly from the original Pali text, to bring these teachings into a modern idiom, replacing some Dharma terms with modern European terms and presenting the stanzas in a Universal way.

When one draws comparisons with the original Pali text, the language is predominantly male. In an attempt to present the text in a more contemporary style, all references of 'he' and 'man' were replaced with 'those' and 'they', so that the text might reflect the oneness of being that is neither male nor female.

The term *Dhamma* (Pali), or *Dharma* (Sanskrit), can perhaps best be described as teachings which express Universal Law or Truth. 'The Dharmas' are the teachings or laws, which uphold and support life and denotes the 'ways' to wisdom, liberation and lasting happiness. The term *Pada* implies the sections, parts, ways or path. So one can say that *The Dhammapada* is: *"The Way of Truth"* or *"The Path of Virtue"*.

The sayings of the Buddha are intended for seekers of the spiritual way. These teachings act as signposts to inspire the unfolding of 'The Self.'

Many of the sayings of the Buddha are concerned with cause and effect, ethics and the practice of mindfulness. The teachings of The Awakened One are simple, yet through mindfulness and direct application in one's life, these teachings can inspire profound insight.

The Dhammapada is perhaps one of the most widely translated Buddhist texts. Standing the test of time, it is without doubt one of the best known and earliest Buddhist scriptures and will remain a constant source of inspiration for generations to come.

The gift of truth surpasses all other gifts and it is my wish that this rendering will be a constant source of inspiration and give you the courage to walk in the footsteps of the awakened and upon the path of peace throughout all your days.

May all that lives be well and happy.

KARMA YONTEN SENGE
LAWRENCE R. ELLYARD

CHAPTER 1

THE CHOICE

1
We are what we think.
All that we are arises with our thoughts;
With our thoughts we make the world.
Speak or act with an impure mind
and trouble will follow,
just as the wheel follows
the ox that draws the cart.

2
We are what we think.
All that we are arises with our thoughts.
With our thoughts we make the world.
Speak or act with a pure mind
and happiness will follow,
just as your shadow, unshakeable.

3

"Look how they abused me and beat me,
how they threw me down and robbed me."
Live with such thoughts,
and you will know only hate.

4

"Look how they abused me and beat me,
how they threw me down and robbed me."
Abandon such thoughts,
and you will know only love.

5

Hating can never dispel hatred.
Only love dispels hate.
This is the Universal Law,
ancient and inexhaustible.

6

You too shall die one day –
knowing this, how can you quarrel?

7

How easy it is to indulge in the senses.
Just as the wind blows down
the shallow-rooted tree,
if you act like this you too will be uprooted.

8

The wind cannot overturn a mountain.
The one who is awake,
strong and humble cannot be touched
by the illusions of this world.

9

If a seekers thoughts are clouded
and their actions reckless,
and filled with deceit,
how can such a person
wear the robes of a sage?

10

But the one who purifies the mind,
and is moderate and truthful
in action and speech
is indeed worthy
to walk with the Awakened.

11

Mistaking the false for the real
and the real for the false,
one lives a life filled with desire and falsity.

12

Seeing the false as the false

and the real as the real,
one lives a life of perfect reality
and is in accord with the Law.

13

When beings have weak minds,
they are swayed from this view to that.
Desire floods them,
like rain though a poorly built roof.

14

Those beings whose minds are strong,
their view is secure;
Desire cannot seduce them
nor flood them with distraction.

15

When one indulges in impurity
suffering follows
in this life and the next.
How great is one's sorrow
having seen the wrong that has been done.

16

Whoever follows the sacred way,
will know joy in this life and the next.
How great is their freedom

having seen
the good that has been done.

17

The one who does harm
suffers in this world and the next.
There is suffering when thinking about these wrong
deeds
and even more suffering
when wondering what will happen to them.

18

The one who creates suffering in this world
laments: "I have done wrong";
thus they travel on a path of sorrow.

19

The one who creates happiness in this world
rejoices: "I have done well";
thus they travel on a path of happiness.

20

One who knows but a little of the Way,
yet is pure in motivation,
supports life, and practices the path wholeheartedly
will walk the path of the Awakened.

CHAPTER 2

MINDFULNESS

21

Mindfulness is the way to life.
Thoughtlessness is the way to death.
The one who is mindful is full of life.
The one who is thoughtless is already like the dead.

22

The wise are mindful and awake,
rejoicing in the wisdom of the enlightened.

23

Meditate with mindfulness;
realize lasting joy.

24

The good who act with kindness
are seen by all with eyes of delight.

25

By watching keenly and working well,
the wise build an island
which no flood can sweep away.

26

The foolish surrender to thoughtlessness.
The wise protect mindfulness like a priceless treasure.

27

Never sleeping, always awake,
the wise meditate with careful attention
and discover true happiness.

28

Those who overcome delusion and
careless behaviour are free from sorrow.
Gazing upon the foolish and ignorant,
they see the churning ocean of sorrow.

29

The mindful among the mindless,
awake whilst others dream.
The one who is aware advances like a racehorse
surpassing all who falter.

30

Through mindfulness,
the seeker surpasses all gods.
How wonderful it is to watch,
how foolish it is to sleep.

31

The seeker who concentrates on mindfulness,
advances like a fire, consuming ignorance in their
path,
leaving nothing but minds pure radiance.

32

The seeker who rejoices in mindfulness,
sees the danger of delusion.
Guarding against harmful ways,
the path of liberation is realized.

CHAPTER 3

THE MIND

33

Just as the fletcher straightens arrows,
so the seeker straightens the unsteady mind.

34

Our minds are like a fish out of water,
thrashing and throwing about.
How our thoughts tremble,
when trying to shake off craving and desire.

35

Wandering here and there,
The mind grasps whatever it desires.
How good it is to tame the mind,
How great it is to master.

36

Yet how elusive is the mind,
how subtle is its way.
So hard to see, the seeker is still,
attentively watching and understanding the minds'
desires.

37

Put a bridle on your wandering mind.
Halt your thoughts, subdue their waywardness,
and you shall find peace.

38

But how can a wandering mind know peace,
if disturbed by doubt and fear?
Without the proper teachings
the true path is obscured from view.

39

A mind that is fearless,
untroubled and calm,
no longer struggles.
Beyond judgements, no fear resides.
A mind like this understands the Way.

40

Observe this body:
how fragile it is, like a glass vase.
Yet build a solid mind,
and one is like a fortress,
able to conquer delusion
and protect what has been won.

41

For soon this body will be cast aside,
lifeless and hollow,
like a useless burnt-out log.
Then what does it know?

42

A mind out of control will do more harm
than two warriors engaged in battle.

43

A mind in control creates more good,
even greater than the love
a mother has for her child.

CHAPTER 4

FLOWERS

44

Who will transcend this world?
Who will conquer death - and heaven too?
Who shall discover the true and shining way?

45

You will!
Just as the gatherers of flowers
find the most beautiful and rare,
so you shall gather the teachings
and transcend this world.

46

Know that your body is merely
the foam on the crest of a breaking wave,
unreal as a mirage.
Break the flowery arrows of craving
and then you shall escape
the king of death and travel beyond.

47

The flowers of pleasure distract the careless,
consuming their world.
They are swept away by death,
like a flood that carries off a sleeping village.

48

The careless ones gather flowers of pleasure.
Never satisfied with one,
they are overtaken by death
before the field is harvested.

49

When the bee gathers honey,
it does not spoil the beauty
nor scent of the flower.
Just so: settle your mind, then carry on.

50

When you remark on the faults of others,
first look at your own.
"What have I done or left undone?"

51

Like the beautiful flowers
which are rich in colour,
yet have no scent,
so are the impressive words
of those who promise, yet do not act.

52

Like the beautiful flowers
which are rich in colour and fragrance,
so life is enriched by those
who say and act in accord with the shining way.

53

Like the countless garlands woven
from endless fields of flowers,
fashion your own life
with innumerable good deeds.

54

The fragrance of sandalwood
and jasmine do not travel far,
but the fragrance of virtue travels in all directions,
even to the ends of this world.

55

How much sweeter than the scent
of sandalwood and jasmine
is the fragrance of good deeds.

56

The scent of lotus flowers
drifts along the morning breeze,
but the fragrance of goodness
rises to heaven.

57

Craving can never block the path of the virtuous.
Their brightness sets them free.

58

How brightly the lotus grows
out of the muddy waters.
Its sweet fragrance lightens
the hearts of all who see it.

59

Just so: awaken!
Let your light outshine the darkness.
Unfold the sweet scent of
your wisdom for all to see.

CHAPTER 5

THE FOOLISH

60

Long is the night for the
one who cannot sleep;
longer still is the journey
of the weary traveller.
How long the wandering
of many lives for the fool
who misses the way.

61

If on the journey one cannot find
a wise companion,
then better to journey alone
than have a fool for company.

62

The foolish think to themselves,
"This is my child, this is my wealth".
But how can the foolish
have wealth or possessions,
when the clarity of their own mind
has eluded them?

63

The foolish who know themselves as fools
have at least some wisdom.
For fools who think themselves as wise
are truly foolish.

64

The spoon cannot taste the soup.
Just so, a fool may live in the
company of the wise
yet still miss the way.

65

But when the mindful know the wise,
even for a short time,
they will understand and taste the teachings,
just as the tongue experiences
the taste of the soup.

66

The foolish are their own worst enemy.

Their sour deeds are their undoing.

How bitter the fruits of their wrongdoing.

67

Foolish deeds bring great remorse.

Why bring tears upon yourself?

68

Do only what you will not regret

and know only joy.

69

Mischief to fools is as sweet as honey,

until the consequences

of their actions turn sour.

Then how bitterly they suffer.

70

For months the fool may fast,

eating only from the tips of grass blades.

But outer rituals count for nothing

for those who simply see the truth.

71

Fresh milk takes time to curdle.

So a fool's actions take time to ripen,
just as surely as a person is burned
when standing on smouldering coals,
hidden in the ashes of a fire.

72

Truly the foolish use their gifts in foolish ways.
They destroy what good is in them
and their own happiness too.

73

The foolish strive for recognition
and power over others.

74

"Let everyone praise me
and look to me for direction."
Such is the strength of their delusion,
such is the swelling of false pride.

75

The path of recognition
and the path of the Awakened
are different.
Look not for recognition,
but follow the path of humility
and set yourself free.

CHAPTER 6

THE WISE

76

The wise will reveal where you have fallen
and where you are yet to fall,
like revealers of a hidden treasure.
It is good to know the wise.

77

Let the wise prevent harm
through the teachings of the way.
The bad may envy the wise,
but the good will praise them.

78

Like the wise,
find the fellowship
of those who love truth.

79

The wise delight in truth.

Their minds are at peace,

following the way of the Awakened.

80

Farmers channel water to their land.

Fletchers straighten their arrows.

Carpenters turn wood,

just as the wise shape minds.

81

A storm cannot shake the mountain.

Neither praise nor blame can move the wise.

82

The wise know clarity,

they hear the truth.

They are like a lake, pure, tranquil, and deep.

83

Clinging to nothing,

the wise walk on.

They are neither elated by happiness,

nor cast down by sorrow.

84

The wise do not prosper
from the misfortune of others,
nor crave for wealth,
kingdom or any other kind of success.
The wise do not rise unjustly.

85

Few cross the river to the furthest shore.
Many are stranded,
running up and down the river bank.

86

The wise,
who carefully follow the way,
cross the river of sorrow,
beyond the grasp of death.

87

Leaving the way of darkness,
the wise walk the way of light.
Leaving the security of ignorance,
the wise seek a higher way,
though knowing the path is difficult to tread.

88

The wise are free from attachment,
free from possessions,
free from the dark places of the heart.

89

Their mind full of concentration,
with the highest regard for the truth,
the wise cling to nothing
and become a light unto themselves,
pure, shining, and free.

CHAPTER 7

THE SAGE

90
At the end of the Way
the sage is free from desire and sorrow,
having broken off the chains that bind.

91
Those who are awake never look back.
They rise like a swan from a lake,
never resting in one place.

92
Those who understand
the illusion of reality
fly an invisible course,
like that of birds in the air.

93

The ones who are free
of this world want nothing.
They are clear and focused.
Like migrating birds,
they leave no trace of a track in the sky.

94

Even the gods admire the
Awakened who has gone beyond.
Free from pride and obsessions
the sage is like a charioteer
who has tamed wild horses.

95

Free from death and rebirth,
yielding like the earth,
clear like a lake,
still as a stone,
the sage is free.

96

With thoughts of stillness,
words of stillness,
the mind of the Awakened
is peaceful.

97

The one who has touched the infinite,
who has cut all ties,
is free from attachment and rises.

98

Wherever the Awakened dwell
there is joy,
be this in the city,
the country,
the valleys or hills.

99

They delight even in the empty forest,
for the Awakened want nothing
and know only joy.

CHAPTER 8

THE THOUSANDS

100

Better than a thousand meaningless words
is one word which brings peace.

101

Better than a thousand hollow verses,
is the one verse which brings peace.

102

Better than a thousand hollow lines,
is that one line which is in accordance
with the law, bringing peace.

103

Though a person may conquer
a thousand people, one thousand times over,
the one who conquers oneself
is the greatest of warriors.

104

The conquest of oneself
is better than the conquest of others.
Then victory is won.

105

A victory like this
can never be denied,
neither by gods nor demons
in heaven or hell.

106

Homage paid to the one
who has achieved self mastery
is worth more than a thousand
offerings or a thousand treasures of gold.

107

Honouring the one
who has achieved self mastery,
even for a single moment,
is worth more than a hundred years
of tending shrines in a sacred place.

108

Those who give gifts for glory
or recognition accumulate no merit.

There is no comparison to the merit
gained by honouring the just.

109

Revering those who, through
old age, have gained wisdom
brings rewards fourfold:
long life, beauty, happiness and strength.

110

Better than a hundred years of mischief
is one day spent in contemplation.

111

Better than a hundred years of ignorance
is one day spent in reflection.

112

Better than a hundred years of idleness
is one day spent with determination.

113

Better to live one day
understanding impermanence
than to live a hundred years
without knowing the truth.

114

Better to live one hour
seeing a path beyond
than to live a hundred years
blinded to the truth.

115

Better to live one moment
completely awake than to live
a hundred years in ignorance.

CHAPTER 9

TROUBLE

116

It is better to do good than harm,
and better to do good at once.
For if you are slow
the mind, delighting in mischief,
will seize you.

117

Turn away from mischief,
turn again and again
before sorrow befalls you.

118

Learn to do good
and do it again and again.
Happiness will follow
and will fill your heart with joy.

119

Fools are happy just so long
as their mischief has not ripened,
but when it bears fruit,
sorrow is the swift result.

120

Even the good may suffer
whilst good actions ripen,
but when these fruits ripen,
the sweet taste of happiness abounds.

121

Do not underestimate the power of darkness,
saying "It cannot happen to me".
Just as water fills the pot, drop by drop,
you can be filled to the brim with folly.

122

Do not belittle your own good deeds,
saying, "I do not deserve this".
Just as the water of virtue fills the pot,
drop by drop, positive merit grows
with each good action.

123

Let the wise avoid trouble,
just as the travelling merchant
avoids a dangerous road.

124

The one who bears no wound
on their hand can touch poison
and will not be harmed.
There is no harm that can come
to the one who does no harm to others.

125

Like dust thrown against the wind,
trouble falls back upon the fool
who harms the harmless.

126

Some are born into this
world again and again.
Some are born into heaven,
some are born into misery.
Those who are free
are born into perfect peace.

127

There is no place to hide
for the one who creates harm,
neither in the sky, the sea,
nor upon a mountain top.
There is no escape from the
consequences of harmful deeds.

128

There is no place to hide
from the inevitability of death,
neither in the sky, the sea,
nor upon a mountain top.
Death will come.

CHAPTER 10

LIFE

129

All who live, fear pain and death.
Knowing you too will die some day,
neither harm nor kill another.

130

All who live, fear pain and death.
See yourself in others
and who can you harm?

131

The one who seeks happiness
by harming those who seek happiness
will never find happiness.

132

For all beings are like you;
they too, want happiness.
Knowing this, never harm another
and happiness will find you.

133

Never speak harsh words
either to yourself or another.
For harsh words return
and trouble is the result.

134

Be still and silent,
like a broken gong.
Know the stillness of freedom,
where striving ceases.

135

Like a herdsman who drives
his cattle to pasture,
so old age and death
will drive you before them.

136

But the foolish, led by the hand
of mischief, forget this
and light the fire that consumes them.

137

If you harm the harmless
or hurt the innocent,
you will fall again and again,
ten times over.

138

If you harm, you will know torment,
suffering, injury, disease and madness.
Knowing this, how can you harm?

139

If you harm you will know loss
of loved ones, loss of wealth and possessions;
you will be a target of persecution
and fearful accusation.
Knowing this, how can you harm?

140

Fire from heaven will strike
you down and upon your death
you will fall into darkness.
Knowing this, how can you harm?

141

Not nakedness, nor matted hair,
nor fasting, nor sleeping on the ground,

neither rubbing the body with dust,
nor the harshest meditations
can purify those who
have not freed themselves from doubt.

142

But the one who lives purely
and is calm and controlled
in quietness and virtue,
the one who does not harm others,
even if wearing fine clothes,
so long as faith abounds,
a being like this is awake.

143

Yet who in this world
is as completely without blame
as a noble horse that rarely feels
the touch of the rider's whip?

144

Like the noble horse
when touched by the whip,
throw off your misery
through faith and wisdom,
understanding the Way
and awakening to the Law.

145

For farmers channel water to their land,
fletchers straighten their arrows,
carpenters turn wood,
so the wise, master themselves.

CHAPTER II

BEYOND LIFE

146
The world is on fire!
Yet you are there laughing,
clouded in darkness.
When will you see the light?

147
Look at your body,
so frail and sick,
riddled with pain.
How can it last?

148
Look at your body,
how frail it is.
It sickens and festers
and surely it fades.
Like all living things,
in the end it sickens and dies.

149

Behold these bleached bones,
this hollow shell
scattered like the dying summer.
Are you still there laughing?

150

Your body is a house of bones,
your flesh and blood for plaster.
Pride lives inside you
as does hypocrisy, old age and death.

151

Just as the glorious chariots
of kings break down,
so your body becomes old.
But the teachings of the Awakened
are changeless and never grow old.
Timeless are these teachings
and forever move throughout time.

152

Those who waste their lives
grow old like an ox.
Feeding on delusion, their size grows,
but not their wisdom.

153

"Through countless weary lives
I have sought the builder of this house
and could not find him.

154

Now, I have found you, O Builder,
and you shall build no more.
The rafters are broken,
the ridge pole is shattered.
I have beaten out desire
and my mind is now free!"

155

For in a lake without fish,
the long legged cranes die.
Those who have squandered their lives
and have accomplished no merit,
perish the same way.

156

As sad as a broken bow,
the foolish having grown old sadly sigh for
the life they have wasted.

CHAPTER 12

THE SELF

157

Love yourself and be mindful,
both day and night.

158

It is wise to know yourself,
before instructing others in self-knowing.
Thus you defeat sorrow.

159

To truly know oneself
is the hardest of disciplines.
To straighten the crooked,
one must first straighten oneself.
Only then can you be a light unto others.

160

It is truly yourself you must depend upon,
for how can you depend on another?
When you obtain a state of self-reliance,
then truly you have found a rare refuge.

161

Just as a diamond can cut
through the very stone which housed it,
so can ones' wrong actions
grind down the peace of one's mind.

162

Those who engage in wrong actions
behave towards themselves as their own worst enemy.
They are like the vines
that choke the very trees which support them.

163

It is easy to engage in activities
that have no lasting benefit,
but it is truly difficult
to do that which is beneficial and good.

164

Like bamboo which dies when it bears fruit,
so fools harm themselves
when mocking the teachings of the wise.

165

All your mischief is yours,
as is all your sorrow,
but virtue and purity are also yours.
You are the source of all your purity
and all your sorrow.
No one purifies another;
it is your own affair.

166

Your work is to discover your path.
Once you discover it,
pursue it with all your heart.

CHAPTER 13

THE WORLD

167

Do not live your live thoughtlessly,
full of distraction and false dreams,
living outside the Law.

168

Awaken!
Rise, be mindful and follow the enlightened way.
Do this with joy through all your days and beyond.

169

Follow the way of the enlightened,
follow the way of virtue,
walk with joy in your heart.
Carry this gift into the world and beyond.

170

See the world as an illusion and a dream.
Do not cling to things of this world,
and then even death cannot touch you.

171

How this world glitters and shines
like a jewelled carriage.
The fools of this world are
seduced and trapped inside.
The wise cannot be fooled.
Having seen, they are set free.

172

The moon emerges from behind the clouds
and illuminates the world.
Just so: overcome ignorance,
and shine forth for all to see.

173

Like the moon that emerges
from behind the clouds,
the one who embraces good
shines forth and turns night to day.

174

This world is shrouded in darkness,

though only few have eyes to see.
They are like birds that have escaped
the cage of ignorance and fly to heaven!

175

See the swans, how they fly towards the sun.
What magic they possess!
The pure of heart conquer all armies of illusion
and take flight on the wings of spirit.

176

If you violate the sacred law,
laugh at heaven
and fill the world with lies,
where will your mischief end?

177

The foolish lack generosity
and are barred from heaven,
but the wise find joy in giving
and enter heaven in this world.

178

Yet better than heaven or happiness in this world,
greater than the one who rules all worlds,
is the one who finds truth
and steps upon the path of peace.

CHAPTER 14

THE AWAKENED ONE

179
The Awakened One,
whose victory cannot be turned into defeat,
has conquered the passions of this world,
and has won.

180
The Awakened One knows no bounds.
With eyes open, the path is free.
By what path can the wise be led astray?

181
The world cannot reclaim
those who are awakened,
nor lead them to distraction.
Even the gods long to be like
those who are free from illusion.

182

It is hard to be born into this world
and even harder to live the life of a human.
Yet it is harder still to hear of the path,
and even harder than this to awaken,
to rise and to follow the sacred way.

183

Yet the teachings of the Awakened are simple:
"Cease to do evil, learn to do good, and purify your
mind."

184

Practise patience,
harm no one,
so say the Awakened Ones.
Profound liberation is the supreme goal.

185

Offend no one,
either by word, action, or deed.
Eat with moderation,
live in your heart
and seek to know your mind.

186

The rain could turn to gold,
yet still your craving would endure.

187

The wise know that
sensual pleasures are impermanent.
Even the gods in Heaven end in dissatisfaction.
Celebrate in awakening and know lasting joy.

188

Driven by fear,
one may seek refuge upon mountain tops
or in forests.
Some take shelter among sacred places
or in shrines.

189

But these are not safe refuges;
they are not refuges that can deliver freedom
from sorrow.

190

Those who take refuge in the Way
find a secure refuge.
Those who travel this path
clearly see the four great truths.

191

Sorrow, the causes of sorrow,
the ceasing of sorrow,

and the eightfold noble path
that leads to the end of sorrow-
this is the way of truth.

192

Then one finds safety;
sorrow is gone
and one is delivered
to a path of freedom.

193.

The Awakened Ones are few in number
and harder still to find.
Blessed is a household
where an Awakened One is born.

194.

Blessed is the birth of the Awakened One.
Blessed are the teachings of the Way
and those who follow.

195

Whoever reveres the one who is awake
and follows the teachings
will cross the river of sorrow
and be free from fear.

196
Revering the Awakened
and the Noble Path,
the seeker lives in peace,
knowing only love and joy.

CHAPTER 15

HAPPINESS

197
Live happily, live with love.
Be free from hatred,
even among those who hate.

198
Live happily, live in health.
Be free from ill-health,
even among those who are sick.

199
Live happily, live in peace.
Be free from greed,
even among the greedy.

200
Live happily, live without possessions.
Like the Awakened,
living with love.

201

Victory leads to hatred,
for the defeated suffer.
Be calm and live happily,
beyond victory and defeat.

202

There is no fire like greed,
no crime like hatred,
no sorrow like separation,
no sickness like hunger,
and no happiness like freedom.

203

Craving is the greatest disease.
Disharmony is the greatest sorrow.
When you know this,
enlightenment becomes your greatest salvation.

204

Health is the greatest possession.
Contentment is the greatest of treasures.
Confidence is the dearest of friends.
Awakening is the highest happiness.

205

Look within, be still.

Taste the sweet nectar of peace,

drink the calm of solitude,

abide in the great happiness of the Way.

206

What joy it is to look upon the Awakened.

What greater joy to keep the company of the wise.

207

How long is the road for one

who travels with a fool.

But travelling with the wise,

the seeker discovers their family

and is filled with joy.

208

Follow the Awakened,

the wise, the loving, the discerning and pure.

Follow them, just as the moon follows the path

of the stars.

CHAPTER 16

PLEASURE

209

Those who give themselves
entirely to sensual pleasures and forget the Way
give up the real for the pleasant.
Caught by the senses,
they lose their way and
later envy those who know the truth.

210

Let the seeker of the Way be free from pleasure.
Let the seeker of the Way be free from pain.
Losing that which you love brings sorrow,
and holding onto the pain of your loss
brings even greater sorrow.

211

Be not bound by pleasure or pain.
Free yourself from attachment to dear ones,

harbour no aversion to those afar.
Release the ties that bind you and know freedom.

212

From attachment springs grief;
from attachment springs fear of loss.
But, if one is free from attachment, there is no sorrow,
so how can there be fear?

213

Becoming lost in affection brings sorrow;
becoming lost in affection brings fear.
But, if one is free from affection, then sorrow ceases,
so how can there be fear?

214

Becoming lost in pleasure brings sorrow;
becoming lost in pleasure brings fear.
Be free in your experience of pleasure, and sorrow
ceases,
so how can there be fear?

215

Becoming lost in desire brings sorrow;
becoming lost in desire brings fear.
Be free in your experience of desire, and sorrow ceases,
so how can there be fear?

216

Becoming lost in craving brings sorrow;
becoming lost in craving brings fear.
Be free in your experience of craving, and sorrow
ceases,
so how can there be fear?

217

Those who speak and live truth
are respected wherever they go.

218

The one whose mind is awake
is free from craving and desire.
The one who has awakened has crossed the river of
desire.

219

Just as travellers who have journeyed long,
who are welcomed with joy upon
their safe return by family and friends...

220

So in the same way,
travellers of good deeds are welcomed
by their positive actions in this life and the next!

CHAPTER 17

ANGER

221
Let go of anger.
Let go of pride.
When you are bound by nothing
you cannot fall prey to sorrow.

222
Curb your anger,
just as a charioteer
controls the unruly horse.
Those who lack control
merely hold the reins.

223
Transform your anger with kindness,
your meanness with generosity,
your lies with truth.

224

These three ways lead to liberation:
speak the truth,
give whatever you can,
forgive and relinquish anger's hold.
Do this and you will perfect yourself.

225

The wise harm no one
for they have mastered their body.
They move to the changeless world
and go beyond sorrow.

226

Those who focus upon liberation,
keep watch both day and night.
They train themselves
to overcome harmful thoughts
and go beyond sorrow.

227

This saying is nothing new:
They blame you for being silent.
They blame you for talking, too.
They blame you for saying little.
Whatever you do, they blame you.

228

There never was,
nor will there ever be,
one who is wholly blamed
or wholly praised.

229

But who would dare blame
the one whom the wise
continually praise?

230

Those whose life is virtuous and good,
who shine like pure gold,
even the gods appreciate their lustre.

231

Beware of anger in your body.
Master your body
and anger will subside.

232

Beware of anger in your speech.
Master your speech
and angry words will subside.

233

Beware of anger in your mind.
Master your mind
and angry thoughts will subside.

234

For the wise have overcome
the anger of body, speech and mind.
They are the true masters.

CHAPTER 18

IMPURITY

235

You resemble the withered leaf;
you have death at your side.
The journey ahead is long,
yet you have made no provision.

236

Be a lamp unto yourself
and learn wisdom.
Free yourself from delusion
and you will light the way.

237

Your life is falling away.
Death is at hand.
The journey ahead awaits,
yet still you have spared
not a thought for your journey.

238

Be a lamp unto yourself
and learn wisdom.
Free yourself from delusion
and you will light the way.

239

As the silversmith removes
dust from silver,
remove your own defilements,
stage by stage.

240

As iron is corroded by rust,
so your own mischief will consume you.

241

Sacred verses rust when neglected.
The house is destroyed without repair.
Beauty is marred through laziness
and watchfulness is ruined through heedlessness.

242

When one lacks dignity and generosity
there is impurity in this life and the next.

243

The worst kind of impurity is ignorance.
Free yourself and you will know joy.

244

Life is apparently easy
for the one who lacks shame,
is always arrogant, vain,
meddlesome and corrupt.

245

Yet life is a challenge
for the one who is modest,
pure, thoughtful and upright.

246

Whoever destroys life
disregards truth and abuses the senses.

247

Whoever intoxicates their mind
to the point of heedlessness
destroys their very foundation.

248

Cease this suffering.
Cease your greed and mischief.

249

The one who envies the gifts of others
will never know peace.

250

Cut down the tree of envy
at the roots and enjoy lasting peace.

251

There is no fire like hatred,
no rushing river like craving,
no trap like delusion,
and no snare like illusion.

252

It is easy to see the faults of others.
It is hard to see the faults of your own.
How easy it is to gossip
about the faults of others,
yet hide your own
as a cheat covers a losing hand.

253

When you dwell on the faults of others
you multiply your own.
How far you are
from the end of your journey.

254

The way to liberation
is not in the sky.
The way to freedom
is in the heart.
Know a path of love
and relinquish your minds desire.

255

All things arise and pass away.
In a changing world of impermanence,
the only permanent thing
is the clear light awareness of our mind.

CHAPTER 19

THE JUST

256

If you judge harshly you miss the Way.
The wise view both sides and know justice.

257

The just see all sides,
hear all sides and without haste
wisely observe the Way.

258

Those who fill the air with words
are not necessarily wise.
Their words fall lifelessly to the ground.
The wise, on the other hand, say little.
Their words are fearless
and filled with love,
soaring to the heavens.

259

Though one's knowledge
may be limited,
if one lives in accord with the Way
and remains upright,
one is said to be a practitioner of the Way.

260

Grey hairs do not equate to mastery.
Though years have passed,
one may have grown old in vain.

261

Those who embody maturity
and are truthful in words
and virtuous in conduct
are said to be the true Masters.

262

Good looks and fine words
cannot make a Master
out of the greedy and jealous.

263

Those who have freed themselves
and walk the path of wisdom
are truly attractive to see.

264

Shaving one's head or wearing the robe
does not mask recklessness and deceit.
How can one such as this be considered
worthy of the righteous path?

265

The true seeker has subdued
unwholesomeness both great and small.

266

One is not a seeker
because of outer forms
that identify the way.

267

The true seeker walks
this path with Body,
speaks wisdom with Speech,
and knows purity with Mind.

268

Silence is not a sign
of contemplation
if the silence is a hiding place
for dullness and confusion.

269

The wise know balance and moderation,
the wholesome and the unwholesome.
Like the one who holds the scales,
the wise know balance of the
inner and outer worlds.

270

The seeker harms no sentient being.

271

The true Master abides
not just in ritual,
nor in meditative bliss alone.

272

The true Master relies
on no one thing.
Freedom comes to those
who go beyond.

CHAPTER 20

THE WAY

273

The way is the eightfold noble path.
The truth is the four noble truths.
The Master is free from craving
and has eyes to see.

274

This is the right way,
the way that leads to liberation,
the way that opens your eyes,
the way to follow.

275

The one who knows this path
outwits sorrow.

276

It is you who must make the effort;
the awakened only show the way.

Who will liberate your own mind,
if not yourself?

277

"Everything arises and passes away".
Understand this and find the shining way.

278

"Conditioned existence is sorrow".
Understand this and go beyond sorrow.

279

"Conditioned existence is illusionary".
Understand this and know clarity.

280

Act while you still possess your health.
Arise now! The fool procrastinates,
indulging in fantasy.
Act now! Find the path of peace.

281

Know words of peace.
Know thoughts of peace.
Harm no one.
By these three ways
you will find the Way
and walk among the Awakened.

282

Sit in the world,
sit in sorrow.
Sit in mindfulness,
sit in joy.
You choose your own seat.
Choose the one where wisdom grows.

283

Cut down the forest of craving,
fell desire and know freedom.

284

Indulge only in lust
and your mind is bound
as close as a calf is to its mother.

285

As you would pluck the spring flower,
pluck the arrow of desire.

286

"Here I shall spend the summer
and the winter too".
So the fool makes plans,
never sparing a thought
that one day death will come.

287

Yet death will come.
Idly dreaming,
fools are only concerned
with the mundane world.
Death quickly fetches them away,
like a flood carries off a sleeping village.

288

When death comes,
neither your friends
nor family can help you.

289

Knowing this,
quickly seek the path of wisdom,
the path that goes beyond death.

CHAPTER 21

WAKEFULNESS

290

Lesser pleasures come and go.
Then there is bliss.
The wise give up the first
to achieve the second.

291

Those who find pleasure
in the suffering of others
will never be free from suffering.

292

Those who recklessly
neglect their work,
and who indulge in mischief,
only create further sorrow.

293

The wise are awake
and do no harm.
They work well,
meditate well,
and their obstacles
diminish more and more.

294

Before knowing the way,
a seeker may be riddled
with thoughts of violence and killing.
But now purified,
the seeker is free.

295

The seeker might have killed
the virtuous and holy,
but now, purified from violence,
the seeker is free.

296

Those who follow the way
of the awakened ones
are themselves fully awake.
They dwell in the presence
of true Masters both day and night.

297

Followers of the way
are always awake;
they remember the sacred path
and follow it both day and night.

298

Followers of the way
are always awake;
they remember the fellowship
of those who seek the path
and celebrate it both day and night.

299

Followers of the way
are always awake;
they remember the nature of the body
and contemplate its mystery,
both day and night.

300

Followers of the way
are always awake;
they delight in compassionate activities,
and give both day and night.

301

Followers of the way
are always awake;
they take joy in cultivating
the heart of wisdom,
sharing it freely, both day and night.

302

To live in the world is hard.
To live outside the world is hard.
It is hard to be near those
who offer no companionship.
For those who wander
without a way,
how hard it is to live such a life.

303

The good and virtuous
are welcomed wherever they go.

304

The good and virtuous
can be seen from afar;
like great mountains,
they stand out for all to see.
But the unskilful are clouded
in darkness and remain as hidden
as arrows in the night.

305

To be one with oneself,

to sit, to work, to rest.

What delight,

as if secluded in a beautiful forest.

CHAPTER 22

IN DARKNESS

306
Those who disregard the truth
live in sorrow.
Those who conceal
their mischief live in pain.
These two ways lead to darkness
where sorrow knows no end.

307
If harbouring reckless intentions,
even the one who wears the seekers robe,
will not find freedom.

308
Better to swallow molten iron,
than to live a life of deception
at the expense of the wise.

309

The unfaithful partner gains these four things:
untold sorrows, broken sleep,
loss of honour and endless suffering.

310

Short lived is the delight
of the unfaithful couple,
for soon consequences
bear their awful blow.

311

Just as a blade of grass
can cut the hand if grasped carelessly,
so a life that is badly lived
can injure the seeker of the path.

312

A seeker who is reckless in actions,
perverse in practice,
and who breaks promises made
will never be free from sorrow.

313

Whatever you may do,
do it well.
Work with devotion,

work with effort.
The seeker who hesitates
merely scatters dust upon the path.

314

It is better to do nothing
than to do what causes harm.
Learn to do good,
for what you do, you do to yourself.

315

Like a guarded city,
guard your mind.
Guard it against trouble,
keep your eyes open.

316

Feel no shame
where no shame is due.
Know you are wrong
if you have done harm.
Confuse the two
and trouble will follow.
Wrong views lead to darkness.

317

Those who fear when there is nothing to fear,
and those who travel dangerous roads, knowing
danger is near,
both hold wrong views which lead to sorrow.

318

Hold wrong views,
and what is right
will seem to be wrong.
What is wrong
will seem to be right.
Wrong views lead to darkness.

319

Those who see things as they are
know the difference
between wrong and right.
They follow the true way
and find freedom.

CHAPTER 23

ENDURANCE

320
You shall endure
the harsh words of others,
just as the elephant
endures the arrows of battle.

321
Those who have trained
themselves well withstand abuse
and are trusted by many,
just as well trained horses
are trusted in battle
and ridden by kings.

322

How impressive it is
to see well trained horses.
But even more impressive
it is to see those who have trained
and tamed their minds.

323

Even riding the finest horse
will not carry you to liberation.
It is only by understanding your own mind
that you will reach your destination.

324

The mighty elephant is restless
when captured
and will not eat when bound.
How he longs to be free.

325

Those who indulge in food and laziness,
who sleep all day long
are like oversized pigs.
Spend your life asleep
and you will experience
lifetimes of conditioned existence.

326

Your mind used to wander,
following lust and craving as it wished.
But now you have tamed your mind,
and it no longer wanders.
It is like an elephant tamed by its kind master.

327

Be watchful and resolute,
drag yourself out of the bog of craving,
just as an elephant lifts itself
from a muddy swamp.

328

If, as you travel,
you find a good companion
who is wise and virtuous,
travel together with joy
and overcome the troubles of this world.

329

If you cannot find
a worthy companion,
better to travel alone,
like a king who has renounced
his kingdom or an elephant
that has left the elephant grove.

330

Travel alone
rather than in the company of fools.
A solitary life is better
than a life kept in bad company.

331

It is good to have the company of friends.
It is good to have the freedom
of having few needs.
It is good to accumulate virtue
before leaving this world.
How great it is to end suffering.

332

It is good to be a father.
It is good to be a mother.
It is good to support the sacred way
and to honour the path of the Awakened.

333

It is good to be virtuous.
It is good to have faith.
What great pleasure arises
when no error is found,
and what great joy it is to be free.

CHAPTER 24

CRAVING

334
Craving grows in those
who are thoughtless,
like the vines in a forest.
Being lost in craving
one leaps from tree to tree,
like a monkey searching for fruit.

335
When you indulge
in craving and grasping,
you fertilize the poison of desire,
and sorrow soon grows.

336
As dew drops fall from the lotus flower,
overcome your craving
and sorrow will fall from you.

337

Just as grass is cleared
to make way for new growth,
cut down desire
lest death crush you
as a flood crushes the helpless reeds.

338

If you do not remove the roots,
the weeds of suffering return again and again.
Therefore: remove your craving and the cause.

339

Thirty-six streams rush toward you
like a torrent, the waves of grasping,
desire and lust.
Bathe in these streams of wrong views,
and you too will be swept away.

340

The streams of craving
flow in every direction.
The creeper of desire
weaves and entangles.
When craving arises,
cut the roots
with the sword of insight.

341

If you are immersed in the river of craving,
how can you be free?

342

Craving, when it catches you,
leaves you bound
like a hare caught in the hunters net.

343

If you are bound by craving,
purify your mind.
Banish craving
and escape the net of desire.

344

Having freed yourself,
the path of freedom lies ahead.
Why then do you run back to the hunters net?

345

It is not the bondage of iron that binds you,
or the shackles of rope or wood.
The soft shackles of wealth,
pride and greed bind you to suffering.
Such cravings are harder to break.

346

Yet those who have broken
the bonds of craving
have surrendered
to the true way and know peace.

347

Entangled by sensual craving,
beings struggle to become free.
They are like spiders caught in their own web;
their craving becomes their tomb.

348

Surrender the past,
surrender the future.
Surrender this moment.
Free your heart and
cross the river of sorrow,
beyond time and space,
beyond birth and death.

349

Such troubled thoughts
of obsession and desire!
How you crave the very thing
that causes you pain.
Release your grip,
for desire only binds.

350

Be still and quieten your mind.
Be watchful, and you will see.
Craving subsides.
You cannot be bound.

351

For those who have reached the goal,
those who have subdued desire,
and those who have found peace
will not return to the suffering
of this life, or the next.

352

The ones who are free
from doubt and fear,
who understand words and their meaning,
and who want nothing
shall not return to this world.
This shall be their last body.

353

"I have gone beyond,
I understand all things
and want nothing.
I have come to the end of craving.
Whom shall I call teacher?"

354

The gift of truth is greater than any gift.

The taste of truth is sweeter than honey.

The joy of truth exceeds all joy.

The end of desire is the end of sorrow.

355

Seeking only pleasure and avoiding pain,

the fool walks the razors edge.

How long can a fool maintain balance?

356

Weeds choke the field;

craving poisons the mind.

Free yourself from craving

and harvest the field of joy.

357

Weeds choke the field;

hatred poisons the mind.

Support those who are free from hate

and harvest the field of love.

358

Weeds choke the field;

delusion poisons the mind.

Support those who are free from delusion

and harvest the field of understanding.

359
Weeds choke the field;
envy poisons the mind.
Free yourself from envy
and harvest the field of liberation.

CHAPTER 25

THE SEEKER

360

Master your eyes.

Master your ears.

Master your nose.

Master your tongue.

Become a master of the senses.

361

Master your body.

Master your speech.

Master your mind

in all that you do, say and think.

362

You are a seeker.

Delight in awareness,

in stillness, and in solitude.

363

You are a seeker.

Speak words of wisdom,

do not exalt yourself.

With humility, walk on.

364

You are a seeker.

Delight in truth,

reflect on truth,

live in truth,

and you shall be sustained by it.

365

Do not entertain thoughts of what others have,

nor envy what you do not have.

You are a seeker,

do not lose sight of the way.

366

For even if you have few possessions,

but use them well,

and live your life with moderation,

many will praise your virtue.

367

Devoid of longing for what they do not have,

seekers require no name or form.

368

Let the seeker abide
in love and kindness,
with devotion for the teachings of the way,
reaching the furthest shore.

369

The seeker travels light,
leaving anger and craving behind.
The load is lightened and liberation is near.

370

For the seeker to find freedom,
five bonds must be loosened.
Release: selfishness, doubt,
spiritual materialism, craving and hatred.
Then come five more:
longing for form in this world,
longing for the formless world,
vanity, agitation, and ignorance.
When you have gone beyond these five,
another five will befriend you.
The fine friends of faith,
vitality, awareness, insight, and wisdom.
With the coarse and subtle attachments liberated,
freedom is found.

371

Be careful on your journey
and meditate well,
lest you swallow the red hot iron
of suffering and scream:
"Why am I in pain?"

372

If you are not still,
insight eludes you.
Without concentration,
where is understanding?
Therefore be still,
concentrate, and insight
will rise in you.

373

For stillness breeds insight
and warms the tranquil heart.

374

See this world without beginning or end.
Go beyond duality, with great joy,
see the boundless reality beyond all worlds.

375

Begin your journey
with patience and stillness
and follow the right instructions.

376

Control your senses;
practice equanimity;
live by the sacred law;
have true friends
who support the Way;
live with purity;
live with joy.
Your heart is open
and sorrow finds no hold.

377

Just as old flowers
fall from the tree,
let your lust and hatred
fall from you.

378

The one who is peaceful in words,
actions and thoughts,
and who gives up temptation
becomes a vessel of peace.

379

Examine your mind
with attention to detail;
look within and find peace.

380

You are the Way;
you are the light;
where else could you look?
Take care and attend to your journey.

381

The one who has confidence in the Way,
goes beyond it, and finds the way to lasting joy.

382

Those who find the Way,
light the world.
They are like the moon,
shining bright for all to see.

CHAPTER 26

ENLIGHTENMENT

383
With all of your heart,
cut off the stream of craving.
When you know this, all that you are dissolves
and you know the uncreated.

384
The world is an illusion,
let it dissolve.
Through insight and concentration,
clearly see how things are.

385
Free from all ties,
free from the bonds of existence,
you shall awaken.

386

Free from ignorance and hatred,
free from corruption of the body and mind,
the sage has attained the highest goal.

387

By day the sage shines,
by night the sage shines.
The one who is awake
radiates light to illuminate the world.

388

No longer engaged in mischief,
the sage has given up such thoughts
and trouble cannot find him.

389

The Awakened do not retaliate,
even when provoked.
The Awakened feel only compassion
and the attacker, shame.

390

With complete control,
do not give in to anger.
The more you avoid harm,
the more suffering ceases.

391

Never cause offence
by what you do, think or say.

392

Respect those who are awake
and learn from their example –
who better to guide you?

393

How do we know a master?
Is it by family, caste, matted hair,
or sacred robes?
By their purity and virtue alone,
is a Master found.

394

What is the use of your fine clothes
and spiritual ideas if, within, you are filled with
confusion and without you embellish yourself.

395

Do not concern yourself
with outer appearances;
only the inner landscape
of liberation concerns the wise.

396

You are not born to greatness;
your virtue is earned.
The Awakened own nothing
and want nothing,
such is their freedom.

397

Beyond fear, beyond grasping,
nothing binds the one who is infinitely free.

398

Having cut the ties of hatred,
having unbound the ropes of delusion,
having unlocked the door of ignorance,
the sage sees the truth and goes beyond.

399

An army of insult
cannot overcome
the patience and calm
of a true Master.
What greater ally is there than peace?

400

Never angry, never straying,
always determined, always true,

the Awakened cannot be defeated.
Resting calmly,
they know this is their last body.

401

The Awakened do not cling;
for, just as water falls
from the sides of a lotus leaf,
desire drops away.

402

Having surrendered
the burdens of attachment,
the sage walks free.

403

The Awakened see things as they are,
neither engaging in worldly pursuits,
nor leaving things undone.
Such wisdom is found
in the minds of great beings.

404

Those who are awake require little in life.
Neither straying, nor in need of a home,
the sage, wanting nothing, walks on.

405

The sage never kills a single being,
or harms another,
or causes either to occur.

406

Peaceful among the violent,
friendly among the hostile,
free from attachment whilst others cling,
these are the signs of a true Master.

407

The Master is free
from envy and hatred;
desire falls away,
just as a tiny seed
drops from the tip of a needle.

408

The Masters speech is kind and truthful,
with words of sweet encouragement
to everyone along the path.

409

The Master takes nothing which is not freely given,
regardless of value, size or beauty.

410

With no more desire for things of this world,
the Masters heart is free.

411

Free from doubt and confusion,
understanding all things,
the sages next step is upon
the shore of liberation.

412

Gone beyond judgements and sorrow,
and the pleasures of the senses...

413

Having gone beyond time,
radiant like a full moon,
pure and shining...

414

Having journeyed through countless lives,
through many turnings, good and bad,
now freed from birth and death,
the sage has reached the other shore.

415

No home can contain
the one who is fully awake
and free from worldly life.
The security of a free mind
is now home.

416

With no need to return to sorrow,
the Awakened one leaves birth and death behind.

417

Completely free from attachment,
asleep no more,
the Awakened can no longer
be chained to this world.

418

Nothing in this world
can seduce the Awakened;
craving is banished forever
and cannot return.

419

The Awakened know the meaning of birth,
know the meaning of death,
and long for neither.

420

By virtue and purity
the Awakened see all things.
Their path is invisible
to gods and mortals;
enlightenment is found.

421

The Awakened has come
to the end of the way,
possessing nothing,
wanting nothing.

422

Beyond heaven,
beyond hell,
by virtue of great purity,
enlightenment is reached.

423

The path is complete.
All that had to be done is done;
nothing remains.
The summit is reached
and enlightenment is found.

BIBLIOGRAPHY

The Dhammapada. Edited and introduced by Anne Bancroft. Element.

A Dhammapada for Contemplation. A rendering by Ajahn Munindo.
River Publications.

The Dhammapada. Pali text and translation with stories in brief and notes.
By Narada Thera. The Corporate Body of the Buddha Educational Foundation.

The Dhammapada. The Path of Perfection. Translated from the Pali with an introduction by Juan Mascaro.
Penguin Books.

The Dhammapada. The Sayings of the Buddha. A rendering by Thomas Byron. Sacred Teachings. Bell Tower. New York.

The Dhammapada. The Path of Truth. Translated by The Venerable Balangoda Ananda Maitreya. Revised by Rose Kramer. Parallax Press.

ABOUT THE AUTHOR

Karma Yonten Senge (Lawrence R. Ellyard) is a
Dharma practitioner of the Karma Kagyu Tradition of
Tibetan Buddhism. He is an avid follower of Buddha
Dharma who currently resides in Australia. Everyday
Buddha is his fourth Book.

O

is a symbol of the world,
of oneness and unity. O Books
explores the many paths of wholeness
and spiritual understanding which
different traditions have developed down
the ages. It aims to bring this knowledge
in accessible form, to a general readership,
providing practical spirituality to today's seekers.
For the full list of over 200 titles covering:

- CHILDREN'S PRAYER, NOVELTY AND GIFT BOOKS
- CHILDREN'S CHRISTIAN AND SPIRITUALITY
- CHRISTMAS AND EASTER
- RELIGION/PHILOSOPHY
- SCHOOL TITLES
- ANGELS/CHANNELLING
- HEALING/MEDITATION
- SELF-HELP/RELATIONSHIPS
- ASTROLOGY/NUMEROLOGY
- SPIRITUAL ENQUIRY
- CHRISTIANITY, EVANGELICAL
  AND LIBERAL/RADICAL
- CURRENT AFFAIRS
- HISTORY/BIOGRAPHY
- INSPIRATIONAL/DEVOTIONAL
- WORLD RELIGIONS/INTERFAITH
- BIOGRAPHY AND FICTION
- BIBLE AND REFERENCE
- SCIENCE/PSYCHOLOGY

Please visit our website,
www.O-books.net

SOME RECENT O BOOKS

THE OCEAN OF WISDOM
Alan Jacobs

The most comprehensive anthology of spiritual wisdom available

The first major anthology of this size and scope since 1935, *The Ocean of Wisdom* collects over five thousand pearls in poetry and prose, from the earliest of recorded history to modern times. Divided into 54 sections, ranging from Action to Zen, it draws on all faiths and traditions, from Zoroaster to existentialism. It covers the different ages of man, the stages of life, and is an ideal reference work and long term companion, a source of inspiration for the journey of life.

Frequently adopting a light touch it also makes a distinction between the Higher Wisdom, which consists of pointers leading to the understanding of philosophical and metaphysical truth, and practical wisdom, which consists of intelligent skills applicable to all fields of ordinary everyday life. So Germaine Greer and Hilary Rodham Clinton have their place alongside Aristotle and Sartre.

The carefully chosen quotations make this book the perfect bedside dipper, and will refresh the spirit of all who are willing to bathe in the ocean of the world's wisdom.

Few individuals have as wide an acquaintance with the world's traditions and scriptures as *Alan Jacobs*. He is Chairperson of the Ramana Maharshi Foundation (UK), editor of *Poetry of the Spirit*, and has translated *The Bhagavad Gita* (O Books), *The Principal Upanishads* (O Books) and *The Wisdom of Marcus Aurelius* (O Books).

1 905047 07 X
£19.95/$29.95

THE WISDOM OF MARCUS AURELIUS
Alan Jacobs

The Meditations of Marcus Aurelius have been described as the best book of practical philosophy ever written. The message is simple but powerful; we have a short time on earth, we don't know what is going to happen, and it doesn't matter. It is the best defence available against the problems and stresses of our time. Most translations are literal and arid, but here Alan Jacobs, a distinguished poet, uses contemporary free verse and added metaphors to convey the essential emotional meaning of the text.

Alan Jacobs is Chair of the Ramana Maharshi Foundation UK. He is author of *Poetry for the Spirit, The Bhagavad Gita (O Books), The Principal Upanishads (O Books).*

1-903816-74-2
£9.99 $14.95

GOOD AS NEW
A radical re-telling of the Christian Scriptures
John Henson

This radical new translation conveys the early Christian scriptures in the idiom of today. It is "inclusive," following the principles which Jesus adopted in relation to his culture. It is women, gay and sinner friendly. It follows principles of cultural and contextual translation, and returns to the selection of books that the early Church held in highest esteem. It drops Revelation and includes the Gospel of Thomas,

"a presentation of extraordinary power." Rowan Williams, Archbishop of Canterbury

"I can't rate this version of the Christian scriptures highly

enough. It is amazingly fresh, imaginative, engaging and bold."
Adrian Thatcher, Professor of Applied Theology, College of St
Mark and St John, Plymouth

"I found this a literally shocking read. It made me think, it
made me laugh, it made me cry, it made me angry and it made
me joyful. It made me feel like an early Christian hearing these
texts for the first time." Elizabeth Stuart, Professor of Christian
Theology, King Alfred's College, Winchester

John Henson, a retired Baptist minister, has co-ordinated this
translation over the last 12 years on behalf of *ONE for Christian
Exploration*, a network of radical Christians and over twenty
organisations in the UK

1-903816-74-2
£19.99 $29.95 hb

JOURNEY HOME
Tonika Rinar

Tonika Rinar believes that everybody is capable of time travel.
We can access history as it really happened, without later
exaggeration or bias. We can also heal ourselves by coming to
terms with our experiences in past lives.

Tonika escorts the reader into other worlds and dimensions,
explaining her own remarkable experiences with an easy-to-
read approach. At one level the book can simply be taken as a
series of fascinating experiences with the paranormal,
embracing past life regression, ghosts, angels and spirit guides.
But it also encourages the reader along their own journey of
self-discovery and understanding. A journey in which you can
discover your own connection with the Universe and the many
different dimensions contained within Creation.

Journey Home offers a multitude of insights, and along the way
looks at some of the fundamental questions asked by all cultures

around the world. Where do we come from? Why are we here? What is the point of our life? What happens when we die?

Tonika Rinar is an extraordinary psychic and visionary, international speaker and workshop leader, with 17 years clinical experience in working with people suffering injury and illness. She has been interviewed extensively on radio and TV.

1 905047 00 2
£11.99 $16.95

THE SECRET JOURNEY
Poems and prayers from around the world
Susan Skinner

A gift book for the young in heart and spirit

These prayers, verses and invocations are drawn from many faiths and many nations but they all reflect the same mystery: the mystery our passage from birth, through life, to death. We are born from the unknown. Our life, except perhaps to our friends and family, is a secret journey of joy and sorrow. Our death is shrouded in questions.

In the words of St Paul, "now we see through a glass darkly.." But we *do* see some things, if we respond to the spirit within. Most faiths, personal or communal, acknowledge the inspiration of the spiritual life founded on truth, love and compassion.

This anthology is a small reflection of the inspired and enlightening words that have been passed on down the centuries, throughout the world. They sing to the child within us all, to the spirit which always remains open and free and clear-sighted. In the words of Master Eckhart: "The eye with which I see God is the same eye with which God sees me."

Each reflection is stunningly illustrated in full colour, making this an ideal gift book for the young and anyone starting on the spiritual journey, or seeking images and verses for inspiration and meditation. A map and short introduction to the world religions, along with notes on sources, make it a useful addition to all libraries in homes and schools.

Susan Skinner is an artist who has made a life long study of world religions, working their themes into exquisite images. She lives near Hastings, England.

1 905047 08 8
£11.99/$16.95

IS THERE AN AFTERLIFE?
David Fontana

The question whether or not we survive physical death has occupied the minds of men and women since the dawn of recorded history. The spiritual traditions of both West and East have taught that death is not the end, but modern science generally dismisses such teachings.

The fruit of a lifetime's research and experience by a world expert in the field, *Is There An Afterlife?* presents the most complete survey to date of the evidence, both historical and contemporary, for survival of physical death. It looks at the question of what survives-personality, memory, emotions and body image-in particular exploring the question of consciousness as primary to and not dependent on matter in the light of recent brain research and quantum physics. It discusses the possible nature of the afterlife, the common threads in Western and Eastern traditions, the common features of "many levels," group souls and reincarnation.

As well a providing the broadest overview of the question, giving due weight to the claims both of science and religion, *Is*

There An Afterlife? brings it into personal perspective. It asks how we should live in this life as if death is not the end, and suggests how we should change our behaviour accordingly.

David Fontana is a Fellow of the British Psychological Society (BPS), Founder Chair of the BPS Transpersonal Psychology Section, Past President and current Vice President of the Society for Psychical Research, and Chair of the SPR Survival Research Committee. He is Distinguished Visiting Fellow at Cardiff University, and Professor of Transpersonal Psychology at Liverpool John Moores University. His many books on spiritual themes have been translated into 25 languages.

1 903816 90 4
£11.99/$16.95

GOOD AS NEW
A radical re-telling of the Christian Scriptures
John Henson

This radical new translation conveys the early Christian scriptures in the idiom of today. It is "inclusive," following the principles which Jesus adopted in relation to his culture. It is women, gay and sinner friendly. It follows principles of cultural and contextual translation, and returns to the selection of books that the early Church held in highest esteem. It drops Revelation and includes the Gospel of Thomas,

"a presentation of extraordinary power." Rowan Williams, Archbishop of Canterbury

"I can't rate this version of the Christian scriptures highly enough. It is amazingly fresh, imaginative, engaging and bold." Adrian Thatcher, Professor of Applied Theology, College of St Mark and St John, Plymouth

"I found this a literally shocking read. It made me think, it made me laugh, it made me cry, it made me angry and it made me joyful. It made me feel like an early Christian hearing these texts for the first time." Elizabeth Stuart, Professor of Christian Theology, King Alfred's College, Winchester

John Henson, a retired Baptist minister, has co-ordinated this translation over the last 12 years on behalf of *ONE for Christian Exploration*, a network of radical Christians and over twenty organisations in the UK

1-903816-74-2
£19.99 $29.95 hb

THE GODDESS, THE GRAIL AND THE LODGE
Alan Butler

We're only just beginning to realise that Bronze Age people knew far more about astronomy and engineering than we have given them credit for, that the Goddess religion continued in various forms through Christianity in the worship of the Virgin Mary down to our own time, that small groups of families and brotherhoods of knights have been highly influential throughout European history. In the essentials of knowledge nothing is new, and the icon of this knowledge has been the Grail.

Reading like a thriller, *The Goddess, the Grail and the Lodge* explains why it was adopted and used, how it existed on different levels to different people, and shows what "Grail Knowledge" really was and is.

Alan Butler is a qualified engineer and an expert on Megalithic cultures and the Knights Templar.

1-903816-69-6
£12.99 $15.95